PARENT'S ULTIMATE EDUCATION GUIDE
Seven Secrets of How to Study

Special Edition

Author: Dr. Stephen Jones

PARENT'S ULTIMATE EDUCATION GUIDE
Seven Secrets of How to Study

For information contact:

SAJ Publishing, Inc.

P.O. Box 5178

Springfield, Pa 19064

E-mail: stephenjoness@rcn.com

Web: www.sevensecrets-books.com

Telephone: 866.544.5490 or

610.544.5480

Mobile 610.842.3843

The author and publisher of this book have put forth a high quality book for your consumption. To organize this project special research was conducted to confirm the effectiveness of suggested study strategies. The author and publisher will not be held liable for any incidents that result from the performance of activities specified.

Graphic Design:

First Impressions Design Group

Philadelphia

Text and Illustrations:

Printed in U.S.A.

ACKNOWLEDGMENTS

A variety of people deserve thanks for their contribution to the development of this book. Thanks to my editors K. Bailey Fucanan and Elizabeth A Hoffman, who provided their expertise regarding the content. I would like to thank my wife, Adele, who provided unwavering support. I am thankful to the numerous parents who offered their study tips.

Special thanks to Stephen Jr. and Stephanie, for giving me time to write. Also special thanks to my parents Herbert and Eleanor Jones who taught me the value of education and prayer.

My special thanks to First Impresions Design Group for their wonderful design and graphics.

Acknowledgments

PREFACE

By Rotan E. Lee, Esquire

Reading, writing, and study skills are critical.
Without those skills, children are more likely than not to be unsuccessful in school and in life.

Academic achievement depends upon the continued development of intellectual skills; and, parents serve as important guides in the educational journey

That reality is clear, uncompromising, and compelling.

The bane of illiteracy or marginal literacy cannot be rationalized, shrugged off as a mere trifle, a paltry matter that reflects indifference rather than inability.

That a child can learn is hardly redeeming if he or she does not. Academic underachievement equates to perpetual lack of motivation and lost of self-worth.

A legacy of failure often results. Resolving the issue requires swift and decisive activism, getting involved in the child's learning processes.

Dr. Stephen Jones has developed the means and the method of assisting parents in helping their children grow intellectually, providing both strategy and syntax, and in developing a child's interest and motivation not only to learn, but also to achieve.

Like *MCGuffey's Readers,* which educated five generations of Americans and sold over 130 million copies, the *Ultimate Parents Education Guide* carries on the tradition of quality supportive education, a vehicle that connects parents with learning and children with academic success.

Education demands out-of-the-box invention, demanding the development of independent critical thought. Moreover learning to read, write, and study hardly constitutes an end in itself, but rather a link to connecting the child with a framework for developing a conscious presence in the world.

PREFACE

Continued from page 4

Importantly, academic disengagement derives from a disconnection between the child and the learning process.

Dr. Jones bridges that gap, taking aim at and guiding parents past mediocrity by electrifying the teaching and learning process. He disavows short cuts; and, he encourages discipline and high standards. His approach demands excellence, supplanting the child's "feel-good comfort zone," pushing past his or her perceived limits and, thereby, discovering the living, powerful, dynamic relation between learning and success.

Preface

TABLE OF CONTENT

Table of Content

TABLE OF CONTENT

Here are the 10 benefits of learning how to prepare your student for college:

● *You will uncover scholarships and grants for college -* The cost of college and trade school increases each year, you need more scholarships and financial aid. Helping your child to improve their grades increases their eligibility for scholarships and grants.

● *You will increase your child's chances of gaining admission to college* Admissions officers observe a student's progress beginning with the ninth grade. A parent can help their student to earn better grades in high school by knowing when to get a tutor.

● *Students obtain better jobs -* Students who attend college and complete a degree obtain better jobs and earn a $1,000,000 more over their lifetime.

● *Learn how to create a better study environment -* Parents who learn how to improve their home study environment improve their son/daughters grades.

● *Improve your student's motivation to graduate -* You will learn how to motivate your student's active involvement in school activities.

● *Learn how to improve your students focus -* You will learn how reading can improve your child's chances of remembering important facts.

● *Learn how to form a positive relationship with teachers -* Your student's teachers will look forward to helping you to educate your child at home.

● *Learn how to find money for college -* Learn how to create a effective financial plan. You can begin to save for college without all of the stress.

● *Improve your son/daughter's chances of college success -* You will begin to implement strategies in high school that make the adjustment to college life easy.

Chapter One
PARENTING 101

A LEARNING FRIENDLY ENVIRONMENT
Getting Started

Every parent wants his or her son or daughter to have a successful K-12 school experience. Parents are responsible for helping their student to have successful elementary, middle and high school experiences. It is important that the home environment lend itself to learning. Parents must organize the appropriate resources to help their child to learn. It's important to have a location that is off limits to noise. You may need to actually print up a sign that says "Quiet Study Room" and post it on the door.

Your children should know that you are in favor of them maximizing their ability to learn. You are committed to purchasing a desk, books, computer and other resources that are the tools for learning. Students need to expand their knowledge through the resources that are available to them in their home. A dictionary is a good resource that will help a student to understand terms that are important. Watching television should become an educational experience. Programs watched should focus on history, science and the environment. Many of these programs can be found on the Public Broadcasting System.

Choose something that you and your child can view that causes your child to think and ask questions. You should willingly discuss money, important topics in the news and community affairs. Surround your children with peers who will have a positive influence on their academic goals. Invite their friends to your home and encourage them to form study groups. Serving food always helps. Try to create an environment where learning is a positive experience. There are many resources that you can purchase at bookstores to keep your child excited about learning. Fill your home with hundreds of books about history, politics, science, and nature. Frequently go on a book shopping adventure at Borders, Barnes and Nobles or a thrift store. You can bring the world to your children just by letting them read about other countries.

FAST TIPS
- *Parents must begin by guiding their child's learning experience*
- *Say NO to television time and turn it into reading time.*

Choose A Place to Study

Finding a location to study may sound like a simple task, but in many cases it is not. The place a student studies is a critical aspect of a successful study session. This place should remind a student of past accomplishments in math, science and English. Those particular tests should be posted in their room.

There are several things you can do to make a location a good place to study. The first thing is to choose a spot that everyone knows is off limits to loud noises, like television or radio. Some students think that they should be entertained while they study, however loud noises serve as a distraction to the brain and it will limit your student's ability to absorb information. Studying in a quiet environment will allow your child to maximize his understanding and to enjoy the learning experience. The sooner that a parent institutes a practice of encouraging their student to study in a quiet environment, the sooner the child will develop this habit for life.

Secondly, identify a desk or table in an environment that has good lighting. The eyes are the gateway to learning. Light enables the individual to clearly see the material that they are studying. A dim light can cause a student to strain their eyes, which can result in headaches. Finding the proper location is important to help your child understand that you consider his learning experience a priority. Sometimes you may need to take your son or daughter to the library so that he or she can experience a different type of learning environment. The earlier you take your child to the library, the better the opportunity to help him/her understand that the library is a valuable resource for information when completing term papers and other types of assignments.

FAST TIPS
- *Consistently remind your child to study in a quiet environment.*
- *Visit a library to provide an alternate place for your child to study.*

Resources That Help

Every student should have the appropriate tools for learning. Create or buy a supply closet so that you will have a central place for your children to find their supplies. You should also place bookshelves with different resource books throughout your home. Erasers, pencils, pens, crayons, colored pencils, colored paper, and cardboard should also be on hand. These are things that a student needs to get started. These basic items can be purchased at the local dollar store and should be easily accessible to your child.

Other items include several rulers and highlighting materials that your child can use on special projects. You may also want to go to a specialty store to get items that are useful for projects, such as artificial grass, trees and other art materials. Folders, three ring binders, clear plastic covers, paper clips and other types of clips should be purchased to ensure that the student organizes papers in such a way that the instructor will easily understand them.

Keeping documents organized is an important part of the learning process. Students will be required to write different types of papers throughout the year. Parents should understand that papers should be typed on plain white paper, however there also may be different types of papers required. Make sure your child purchases the appropriate type of paper. A project could require construction paper or even resume paper. All can be purchased at the local store. These resources can help a student give an effective presentation or adequately complete homework assignments. Some other stores you might want to frequent for supplies include Staples, K-mart, Wal-Mart, local dollar stores, arts and crafts stores and hobby shops. At these stores you will find all kinds of creative items for projects that are assigned throughout the year. Projects can account for one third of a students' grade so don't discount the importance of seeking out the best quality materials to help your son or daughter complete them.

PARENTING 101

It is also important to have a reference library in your home. Some of the items you should include are a Webster's dictionary, a thesaurus, a dictionary of synonyms and a dictionary of computer terms. These are all important resources for gathering information concerning any books that your student is likely to read. Don't forget special language books, such as Spanish, French, German and Russian dictionaries. These should be purchased so a student can have an easy understanding of languages and other topics.

Books are vital resources that provide topics for research papers and insight into specific subjects. Specialty books in your home should include books on biology, specifically insects, the human body, reptiles and all kinds of animals. Every family should have no less then 400 different types of books in their home. Places to purchase books abound. Many can be found at a reasonable cost at yard sales, flea markets or used bookstores. Ask friends for old books so that you can expand your child's library.

Reading is an essential skill students must develop. Strong readers are better writers. Writing is a skill that will be required throughout a child's life. A computer is now considered a standard learning tool required for many different types of projects. If finances do not allow for you to have a computer at home then utilize computers at your local library. Look in the Yellow Pages for used computer stores. These stores can offer computers at a reduced price. Ask relatives if they have an old computer that has a basic word processing program that can be used to type papers. New computers can be purchased in just about any electronic or office supply store. Brands include Dell, Hewlett Packard and Compaq. These are all good and can provide access to online materials to help your student.

FAST TIPS
- *Keep at least 400 books in your home.*
- *A new or used computer can increase your student's chances of earning better grades.*

How to Create A Quiet Environment

Establishing a quiet environment starts with everyone in the house understanding the importance of quiet time. Organize a meeting to talk about when quiet time is essential. Everyone must agree on how they will cooperate with the plan. A formal meeting lets everyone know that this is a priority for improving your child's academic performance. Each person has a role to play. Encourage your son or daughter to share how his or her grades have improved since studying in a quiet environment. For many families, the living room, kitchen or bedroom is the place their students study. Students should try to stay clear of times when there are a lot of people or traffic in these rooms. For example, at the dining room table, it is better to take a break and eat dinner then to have major distractions while you study. The brain absorbs information best when there is a quiet environment.

FAST TIPS
- *Emphasize the importance of having a plan to earn good grades.*
- *Help your student to keep their brain active by reading new books each week.*

Chapter One

Keep it Positive

It is important to create a positive environment for your student to learn. A mind that is free of stress and anxiety can retain information better. Both the mind and the body are adversely affected when a student becomes anxious during a studying session. Frustration can set in if the student does not have sufficient information in his notes or textbook. The key is to keep the student's life positive by providing him with the resources and tutoring that he may need to have a meaningful learning experience.

Try to identify academically successful friends, as well as teachers who can have a positive influence on your child. Also, identify a teacher who will help your son or daughter to maximize his or her learning experience. Connect with a teacher who understands your son or daughter's learning style and who can communicate the best way that you can help him or her at home. When a student knows that someone cares about them, they relax and learn information easily. Certain subject areas may also require additional books, compact discs and audiotapes designed to help you student learn more constructively. Your positive attitude can save your son or daughter from having bad experiences and can even improve his or her test scores.

For example, if you tell your child that you don't like mathematics, it could cause him to automatically assume that he can't learn that same subject. So turn your thoughts around about it and don't even communicate the fact that you don't understand mathematics. Find the resources that will help him understand it. It may require a tutor or other individuals in class or it might require direct contact with the instructor to get the best results for your student. Enable the rest of the children in the home to maintain a positive attitude and encourage them to read different types of materials that talk about keeping positive thoughts. Also, look for books about successful leaders who have overcome adversity to accomplish tremendous goals. These types of books can encourage your children to achieve greater success.

Chapter One

PARENTING 101

Parenting 101 Application

ONE As a parent you must view yourself as the teacher who successfully manages the home learning environment. You must be willing to set limits on television viewing and video game playing during the week as well as time spent on the telephone, computer and internet. These are the biggest distractions that most students face. You must say no to these when your student does not perform well on a test. If your student is having a problem, your next step is to talk with the teacher directly and pursue tutoring.

TWO Don't be afraid to say no to the things your child wants when they are not performing well in school. You may need to take away certain privileges, like playing on the basketball team or participating in the marching band. Removing them for a time may seem difficult, but it will pay off when your student starts to achieve better grades.

THREE Parents play a major role in putting the puzzle called education together. There are many things that a parent can do to lay a solid foundation for learning at home and school. Parents must make a commitment to creating a formal study time when your child comes home from school. Studying in the evening should not be acceptable unless the student plays a school sport. When a student studies soon after school they have better recall of what they learned during the day.

FOUR Organize your calendar so that you can attend all parent-teacher meetings throughout the school year.

FIVE Help your student to create a personal entertainment-free study zone. A television or computer can be too much of a distraction for some students. You can set up a fantastic learning environment that is free of distractions. Ask your student to offer some suggestions about items to include in their study area.

PARENTING 101

Parenting 101 Application

SIX   Develop a study plan that includes substantial reading. Spend time talking to your child about the book they are reading. Give your child special attention and an opportunity to see a stage production of the story. You can also have discussions about what lesson the book is trying to teach the reader.

List several books your child will read:

_____
_____
_____
_____

A. Encourage your student to write down the characters from the book and summarize their roles. The review sheet your student creates will act as a resource when they need to report on the book.

SEVEN   Don't wait until the new school year to plan your child's educational experience. If you have questions that were left unanswered after the last school year, arrange an August meeting with his former teacher. Also meet with your student's new teacher to be sure that you know what your student needs. Let's say for example, English is a subject where your student needs help. During August ask his teacher about the availability of tutoring and other resources.

Notes

PARENTING 101

What Parents are Saying
Pastors Terry and Pam Davis

1. Set a high standard regarding your son/daughters performance in each class reiterating those standards periodically.

2. Provide reward incentives for reaching grade and class behavior goals.

3. Sit down with the person who is responsible for creating a class schedule. Make sure that there are sufficient math and English courses in the assigned curriculum.

4. Make sure they get a good night's sleep and eat a full breakfast (not Pop Tarts, etc.) with vitamin supplements every morning. It really makes a difference in how they feel and perform especially before lunch which is when most of their work is done.

5. Study time is immediately after school everyday until all work is complete. If none is assigned then some type of review study or reading is done.

6. All extended work (book reading, projects) should be scheduled and completed early or on time to avoid late and shoddy last minute work.

7. Video games and TV are strictly limited, but not completely eliminated, during the school week.

8. Talk about classes and assignments regularly to make sure they understand and stay on track. If there are any problems spend extra time together in that area and encourage your son/daughter not to be afraid to ask for help in class or say "I don't understand".

9. Weekend homework, when assigned, is done early in the weekend. Because study during the week is enforced pretty strictly, weekends are generally for fun. They need that too.

PARENTING 101

Parenting 101 Summary

1. Keep education as a primary focus of your discussion.

2. Don't set a limit on the amount of resources you will use to prepare your son/daughter for college.

3. Talk with family members who have successfully sent a child to college.

4. Ask your child's teacher for suggested books to read during the summer.

5. Use positive words to raise your child's motivation to learn

6. It's important to begin with the end in mind.

7. Enroll your child in a community college course during high school

8. Don't be afraid to change schools if you do not feel that your student is getting the best education.

9   Visit a local library or book store to let your son/daughter meet an author in person. You can make writers their heroes.

10. Watch educational DVD movies about a history lesson your student is learning in class.

Parenting 101 Activities

1. Sit down with friends who have academically successful children and ask them about their education strategies.

2. Form and select the themes for your student's projects at the beginning of the year.

3. Make a list of distractions preventing your child from studying. Get started by clearing the distractions daily. Create a formal time for your student to study in a quiet environment.

4. Create your own library of books and magazines that will help you to uniquely educate your child. Pursue information on the internet.

PARENTING 101

Next Steps Worksheet

What have you learned?

_____

_____

_____

_____

_____

_____

_____

How will you apply this information?

_____

_____

_____

_____

_____

_____

_____

_____

Chapter One

PARENTING 101

Next Steps Worksheet

What is the first step that you will take?

_____

_____

_____

_____

_____

_____

_____

_____

_____

_____

How will you use this information to help your son/daughter?

_____

_____

_____

_____

_____

_____

_____

Chapter One

Chapter Two

PREPARING FOR STANDARDIZED TESTS

How to Prepare for the Next Test

An important priority for students and parents is performance on tests throughout the year. Tests and quizzes are methods that teachers use to measure students' comprehension of their subjects. You can be supportive by constantly having a positive attitude toward your child. This attitude alone can help your son or daughter to overcome test anxiety. Test anxiety can cause even the best student to lose confidence in their ability to perform well on any type of examination. How do you help your student to overcome test anxiety? The more prepared he feels when its time to take the test the better he will perform. So your job is to help him get prepared. You can ask him questions to determine which resources he needs to be successful. For example, your student might prefer to read notes with other students or maybe he needs to talk directly with the teacher. Another book on the same subject may be needed because the one he uses in the classroom isn't sufficient to provide him with enough information to have success.

Your student may need additional supplies, like a special kind of dictionary or calculator or access to a computer that allows him to conduct research. You will need to check with him periodically to make sure he has everything he needs in the classroom notes. Sometimes a student will need to get together with other students to ensure that the information he has is adequate. I cannot tell you how many students leave their calculators at home before taking examinations. It is important to make sure your student has the tools that he needs. Sometimes teachers assume that they are teaching students who are not interested in their subjects. The better your student performs in the subject and expresses interest, the more likely the teacher will be inspired.

Parents should encourage their students to use a calendar to chart exams for each class. It's never too soon to use a calendar because it helps a student to get organized. A calendar can help a student to plan for an examination and it is a useful resource for getting projects started on time.

PREPARING FOR TESTS

Starting projects a day before it is due can result in an ineffective presentation and a bad grade. Procrastination can be a large barrier to performing well on an examination. Helping your student feel prepared can provide them with the confidence they need to achieve excellence on quizzes, tests and projects.

FAST TIPS

- *Your son or daughter can overcome test anxiety by increasing his or her study time before a test.*
- *Purchase a calendar so your student can map out examinations and projects by date.*

Where are the After School Programs?

Students across the country receive tremendous benefits from participating in after school programs. There are sports programs, community groups, school programs, and religious programs designed to bridge the gap between 4:00 p.m. and 6:00 p.m. when parents are not home. You want to research early to identify possible programs for your child. Learn the purpose of the program and interview the people who will be involved in delivering it. Partner with them and make them aware that you will be supportive and will provide assistance whenever possible. Ask the principal's office or the school guidance counselor about programs that are available.

Specifically ask your son or daughter about his or her interests so that you can find the best program, whether it focuses on music, athletics, dance, business, science, nursing or engineering. There are lists that you can obtain from your local legislative office. Some after school programs require financial resources, others do not. Do your research and sometimes you will also find suggestions in local newspapers.

To give you an idea of different types of programs that may exist in your local community, the YMCA, YWCA, Upward Bound, Inroads, MESA, and Communities in Schools all offer different types of after school programs. There are also programs that emphasize education. Ask about the availability of a tutoring or homework review component. Ask about the goals the program has for its children and obtain those in writing, if possible. You may even be able to offer suggestions about how to make the program better.

FAST TIPS

- *Involve your student in an after school program right away.*
- *Take advantage of tutoring that is offered through these programs.*

PREPARING FOR TESTS

How to Understand K12 Standardized Tests

Every parent must be aware that their student will take a standardized state or private test during their K12 years in school. These tests provide feedback about what the child has learned throughout their enrollment. Due to federal law the results of the standardized K12 tests influence who remains in leadership at certain schools. A school where students are performing below standards could change leadership several times. Your child's performance on the standardized test counts when decisions are made about certain schools continuation. Therefore, each parent and student must take these tests seriously. You can play a tremendous role by consistently helping your child to prepare for the test.

How to Prepare Your Student for K12 Testing

There are several things you can do to prepare your student for the test. Make sure that he/she is actively participating in the test preparation. Most schools spend several weeks preparing their students for the test. Teachers talk about the types of questions and how to get the best results. Make sure that you reinforce the importance of the test. You can ensure your students success by helping them to get sufficient rest weeks prior to the test. During the week of the test send your student to bed earlier than normal.

Provide a healthy meal each morning. Ask your school for the results of the test so that you can get a sense of how your child is learning and what you should do to facilitate their continued academic growth.

PREPARING FOR TESTS

SAT Preparation Strategies

 The SAT test is an extensive one day examination that colleges use to measure students potential to succeed at college. Your student will take the PSAT first which are the preliminary 10th grade test and the SAT in the 11th or 12th grades. The SAT has three sections verbal, math, and the written component. Each student automatically earns 200 points per section for signing their name. Each section of the test is worth 800 points. This means that the highest score that a student can accumulate is 2,400 points. I suggest that every student should take a SAT course and buy books to study for the test. Most important every child should spend their days in school gathering new information. The student with the most knowledge of math, science and history will perform better on the test. If your child earns good math grades fantastic. If they struggle with math, I suggest that you get a tutor to work with them throughout their K12 experience. Math is an area of study where many students loose points on the SAT test. Help your child to prepare for the future SAT tests by giving them academic support when they need it.

How to Respond to the Results

The SAT is not the sole measure of whether a student will attend college. There are over 3000 colleges for your student to attend. Keep your child's options open and encourage them to apply to more than four colleges. This will increase their chances of acceptance. Your son/daughter can also take the ACT test, which is another standardized college admission test that some students like better. Students can list their college choices on the SAT form and the copies will be sent directly to the schools they choose. A student can request additional results and mail them to the college of their choice. When your student is finally accepted to a college consider the cost, the amount of financial aid provided, the schools reputation for graduating students and the location of the school. Use the test result as a spring board not the sole measure of your student's chances of success in college.

PREPARING FOR TESTS

Test Preparation Application

Test preparation is an essential aspect of every student's success in school. Some students have never given thought to the importance of preparing for a test. They may study the night before an examination or on the bus on the way to school. Students must develop a different mindset in terms of their personal investment into learning sufficient math reading, writing, math, and computing skills.

1. Have your child ask each teacher the major requirements for his class.

Teacher Requirements_____

Teacher Requirements_____

Teacher Requirements_____

Teacher Requirements_____

Teacher Requirements_____

> A student should organize separate sheets of paper with the major requirements for each class and keep these at the front of each of his class binders. A student who places his priorities on paper usually performs better on tests and is generally more organized as test dates approach.

> The student should complete a calendar of all assignments and place it in a prominent location where it will always be seen. Tell them to get started right away.

2. Your student should go to the library to research other books that can strengthen his knowledge of each subject area. Inspire your student to take the initiative to prepare for each examination at least three days before the actual examination date.

Test Date_____

Test Date_____

Test Date_____

Test Date_____

Test Date_____

PREPARING FOR TESTS

3. There are several ways that you can support your son's or daughter's study time. The most important is to create a quiet study environment.

4. Your student should begin his preparation for a test with the right attitude. When your student is prepared he will reduce his stress level.

5. Parents must help students identify distractions that may prevent them from studying. There are many distractions that prevent students from concentrating especially when they don't enjoy a particular topic.

6. Your student can eliminate some distractions by studying in a different location, like the public library, or participating in an after school study hall.

7. Allow your computer to become a valuable test preparation tool. There are many computer software games for math, history, and English that make learning fun. Ask your son's or daughter's teacher if there is something he can recommend.

Create a list of software to purchase.

_____

_____

_____

8. Encourage your student to answer some of the questions at the end of each chapter of his classroom textbook. By doing this he will uncover additional facts that the may not have considered. Some books provide an answer key at the back of the book.

PARENT TESTIMONIAL
Douglas and Linda Coleman

Provide personal tutoring in subjects that require a strong foundation.

Get the proper diet, exercise and rest.

Speak correctly at all times and use proper table manners at all times.

Eat at least dinner together to discuss whatever is on anyone's mind about school, play or work.

Going to church as a family; exposure to believing in God; participate in church activities; give some of your money to church.

Remind them that material things are rewards for good works and not just because.

Give less gifts at Christmas and more for good grades and unselfish acts of kindness.

Bad grades can and do result in the repetition of a grade and limit your options for furthering your childs education.

Encourage your student to hang around with children who are even smarter then they are and interested in positive things.

Test Taking Summary

1. Prepare for every test at least 3 to 5 days before it is time to complete the examination

2. Create a plan that allows your student to have quite time to study in you home.

3. Using your classroom books and other books from the library will give your son/daughter a complete understanding of your instruction.

4. Get your son/daughter ready for tutoring sessions prior to meeting in a study location

5. Arrange a study time that allows your student to maximize the knowledge you absorb.

6. Ask your son/daughters instructor for advice about how to prepare for the next test.

7. Get to know several students in their class who are doing well and arrange a study session

8. When you are completing math problems make sure that all of the numbers line up.

Test Preparation Activities

1. Help your son or daughter create a multiple-choice test by reviewing questions at the end of the chapters. Create a game where they earn a nickel for each correct answer.

2. Ask your student to create a list of textbook words that he does not understand. Go to a dictionary or the Internet to find the definition. Understanding the meaning of words will help your student to perform better on tests.

3. Talk about test anxiety that your student may be experiencing in math, history or another subject. Help your child to relax by asking him to slowly breathe in and out 10 times. This exercise will cause the body to relax so the mind can think more clearly.

4. Develop a list of tutoring resources to use if your student is having trouble. You can contact local colleges or your local high school. Some community groups also offer tutoring.

Notes
_____

Next Steps Worksheet

What have you learned?

_____
_____
_____
_____
_____
_____
_____

How will you apply this information?

_____
_____
_____
_____
_____
_____
_____
_____
_____
_____

Chapter Two

PREPARING FOR TESTS

Next Steps Worksheet

What is the first step that you will take?

_____

_____

_____

_____

_____

_____

_____

_____

How will you use this information to help your son or daughter?

_____

_____

_____

_____

_____

_____

_____

_____

_____

_____

_____

Chapter Two

Chapter Three

WHERE'S THE MONEY

Where's The Money For College?
How to Get Started

Many parents think that starting to save for college while a child is in elementary school is too early. It is never too early to start a financial plan to pay for college. Getting started does not require a lot of money, but it does require a plan. First, write down all of your monthly bills. Which should include housing, electric, gas, water, clothing, food, etc. Writing them down will give you a clear picture of how much your expenses are each month. Write down the amount of money you earned this month and subtract your expenses from it. This will let you know how much you have to start saving for college.

You should compare your monthly debt to your income to determine how much you can invest at a later date. You might want to start a college account that will allow you to save money freely. You can start with $25 dollars, which may seem like a little investment, but over time it can grow into a large amount. Just as your salary increases so can your monthly investments. All parents learn to save a little at a time. This account should have a sole purpose: saving for your child's college. There are many vehicles for saving money. Some states have accounts that allow you to invest for a certain college in the state, at today's tuition cost. They are called 529 investment plans.

Investigate all of the policies regarding your 529 account in your state. It is important to know that there are penalties if your child should attend college early or if your son or daughter decides to attend college out of state. Do not limit yourself to the plan offered in your state. There may be different 529 plans in a nearby state. You can find out about these accounts by discussing them with someone who works in the financial aid department at a local college or your state office for financial aid.

WHERE'S THE MONEY

Another place to find out about college savings plans is at your credit union or bank. Each offers different types of plans and they can take the money from your account according to your instructions. Depositing your money electronically allows you to begin earning interest right away. Don't limit yourself to a college savings plan because there are many other types of accounts where you can save even more money for college. You should see your money grow over time. The important thing to remember is that there is money for college out there and you must continually gather information. There is over $90 billion in scholarships available every year. You should establish a binder that you can keep adding information to throughout the year. It should include articles you have read from magazines or newspapers, information you have heard over the radio and received in the mail or information from a college fair you attended. College fairs are great sources of financial aid information.

Another good place to find books about scholarships is at the library. Most libraries have entire sections of scholarship books, available for virtually everything. There are scholarships for left-handed people, musicians, poets, artists, athletes, community volunteers, academic performance, and low-income. Don't limit the types of scholarships your child applies for. Ask your student to write a standard letter about why he should receive a scholarship. The letter should include the following: why he values college, what major he has selected and why, what he's been doing in high school and his future goals. It is important that your student write this letter right away because scholarships have deadlines. There is plenty of money available, but obtaining it requires work. It is important to have an organized scholarship plan.

FAST TIPS
- *Start saving for college this week.*
- *Start an account with minimum of $ 25.00.*

WHERE'S THE MONEY

Pursuing Money For College

Did you know that you could start your own campaign to raise money for your son or daughter to attend college? I've noticed that many schools ask students to write letters to family members asking for contributions for the cost of a trip to another country. Students are able to raise thousands of dollars by asking family members, friends and contributors to donate money toward their trip. Your child can write a letter telling the reader he is about to attend college, the major he's selected and why he values the opportunity to attend school. He can then ask for a contribution. Send this letter to family, friends, co-workers and local stores. Frequently you will get more than you expect.

The letter should let everyone know the amount of money your child is attempting to raise. Remind the reader that the cost of college can range from $12,000 to $40,000 a year. Including this information gives them a better perception on how much it costs to attend college. Encourage your church to start a scholarship fund. Go by your local politician's office and leave a copy of your letter asking the staff to participate.

FAST TIPS
- *Help your student to write a letter requesting scholarship support. Get your local politician involved.*

Talking to the Financial Aid Office

There are a lot of things you can do to benefit from the resources that are available in the college financial aid office. The first step is to get over the fear that no one is willing to help you. Don't wait until your son or daughter is in his or her senior year of high school to schedule an interview with a local financial aid office. Try several different schools to determine which one is really interested in helping your child to complete his college degree. Call four-year colleges and two-year colleges and compare the different costs. Set up an appointment and follow through with it. If you are unable to make your appointment, call the office and reschedule.

WHERE'S THE MONEY

There are several questions to ask the financial aid officer. When you have an organized list of questions you ensure that you will obtain the primary information that you came to receive. Here are some questions you should ask: How long does it take to process a financial aid package? Do you have a list of scholarships or websites I should visit? What family expenses do you consider when determining a student's financial aid package? When is the best time to turn in the financial aid form? Are there additional sources of money available, not offered through the financial aid office? Do in-state students receive greater assistance then those from out-of–state? Are there any local financial aid meetings that I should attend? Are their any sororities or fraternities that offer scholarships? Can a student's financial aid package change from year to year? How long does receiving a new scholarship effect a financial aid package overall?

One advantage to visiting a financial aid office is to give you a different prospective on the money offered to students. Remember to bring a composition notebook so that you can keep track of your discussion. Also, ask for a business card so that you can ask additional questions later via email. Remember that you can control the financial aid process. You must obtain the maximum amount of financial aid that your child is eligible to receive. Follow through with meetings with the financial aid office when your student is in college. You can save yourself a lot of heartache just by taking control of the financial aid process. It will require a lot of effort, but it will be worth the pay off by limiting the amount of debt that your son or daughter incurs when he or she leaves college.

FAST TIPS
- *Create a series of questions you will ask a financial aid officer*
- *Be prepaired to meet all financial aid deadlines by writing the deadline dates on your calendar.*

WHERE'S THE MONEY

College Financial Planning Applications

There are several things that you can do to ensure a smooth financial future. One strategy that really works is saving 10 percent of your salary. When you save for unexpected events, such as a pipe leak or car problems, you avoid the headache of using a credit card with a 20 percent interest rate. You must write down your overall budget on paper. If your money grows by 5 percent each year it should rise with the cost of college tuition.

Talk to at least two bank representatives about their college savings plans. Make a list of two banks you will visit.

_____

_____

Always ask your bank if it is giving you the highest interest rate. There are several ways that you can save for school and college expenses. The big drawback is that your investments may be taxed. College savings plans are not taxed right away, unless you make an early withdrawal. You can invest in money market accounts, certificates of deposit, savings accounts and stocks. You may want to diversify your investment among the college savings plans and other savings accounts. Seek help from the experts who can help you to sort out all of the options.

Conduct a little research before you meet with a financial planner. When you start your research, you may find banks that have better interest rates. Make a list of potential banks.

_____

_____

_____

WHERE'S THE MONEY

It is important to teach your children the value of money while they are young. You can help them to form good habits for life. Also, teach your student the value of delayed gratification. When you don't give your children everything they want when they want it they learn to control their spending. Let your student open up a savings account. Periodically review the account with your student so they can see how it grows.

Create a plan to save money and invest it in your child's education. When you use coupons when you're shopping and you insulate to save on your energy expenses, you are in a better position to save money.

Try having fun with your son/daughter by playing games that use play money. One of the most popular money games is Monopoly. It is a game that demonstrates how an individual can acquire and lose property. There are also games that reward participants based on the decisions they make about money. It's good to observe how your student makes decisions regarding purchases.

Talk with your student about how to make good financial decisions when they are in college. Most students do not go to college with hundreds of dollars to spend.

Students who have an interest in attending college should start to gather scholarship information during their ninth grade. Uncovering scholarships during the senior year is easier when you've gathered scholarship materials early. You should purchase a three-ring binder and put all of you're your information into the binder according to the month the application is due. Try to complete applications at least a month before the deadline. When you receive some of the applications ask your student to prepare a response in writing to a specific question on the application.

WHERE'S THE MONEY

Here are a few example questions from an online university scholarship application:

● What are your career goals and how do they fit with the mission of our college?

● Describe a difficult problem that you've faced recently and had the strength to resolve.

● Why do you believe that you will be the best student for our college?

You will be surprised how fast 12 years of school goes by and then you need money to send your child to college. You are setting yourself up for failure if you wait until next year to start saving money for college. I recommend starting a college savings plan with $25. You can always gradually increase your monthly contributions to this account.

Notes

WHERE'S THE MONEY

What Parents are Saying

Gregory Davis, CLU, ChFC, CFP, RPA
Vice President, Lincoln Benefits Group

1. Begin your search for scholarships during the ninth grade.

2. Apply for admission at six or eight colleges so that you can maximize your financial aid options.

3. Complete the Free Application for Federal Student Aid (FAFSA) as soon as it is released. Usually the application is available at the beginning of January.

4. Plan your financial aid strategy by investing in a 529 college saving plan. You can learn more at savingforcollege.com or consider a contact with Coverdell funding plan.

5. Talk to the financial aid officer at all of the colleges you select. Your goal is to ask for information about hidden scholarships.

6. If you don't like the financial aid package you've receive contact the financial aid office and request additional funding

7. Don't make the assumption that private colleges will always cost more than public colleges. Apply for admission to different types of colleges.

8. If you are the first person in your family attending college there are special scholarship.

9. Remember the federal government offer funding information at http://studentaid.ed.gov. Also, you can try Fastweb.com it has a comprehensive scholarship website.

Chapter Three

WHERE'S THE MONEY

Money Summary

1.   Gather information about scholarships and grants beginning with the 9th grade.

2.   During the second semester of the 11th grade start the process of filling out scholarship applications. Create a list of dates when all applications must be submitted.

3.   Talk to a financial planner they are experts regarding how to save money for college.

4.   Don't be afraid to ask family to support your child who will be attending college. Students are eligible to receive scholarship support from family.

5.   Consider starting a family scholarship foundation for students who are attending college or a trade school.

6.   You can ask your school counselor about scholarship information.

7.   Meet with your local state representative to uncover grants that your state offers.

8.   Ask your teachers for letters of recommendation during the 11th grade. Ask them to leave out the date.

9.   Research on the internet companies that offer scholarships and internships.

10.   Enter contests that offer scholarships to the students who win.

Managing College Finances Activities

1. Sit at home and make a list of places where you purchased items and saved money. Put that savings into your child's college account.

2. Discuss which bank in your area provides the best service. Establish a college savings account there.

3. Organize a list of potential jobs on a college campus by visiting college employment offices.

4. Help your student to develop a sample cover letter to use with scholarship applications.

Notes

Chapter Three

WHERE'S THE MONEY

Next Steps Worksheet

What have you learned?

_____

_____

_____

_____

_____

_____

_____

_____

_____

How will you apply this information?

_____

_____

_____

_____

_____

_____

_____

_____

_____

_____

_____

_____

_____

Chapter Three

WHERE'S THE MONEY

Next Steps Worksheet

What is the first step that you will take?

_____
_____
_____
_____
_____
_____
_____
_____
_____
_____

How will you use this information to help your son/daughter?

_____
_____
_____
_____
_____
_____
_____
_____
_____
_____

Chapter Three

Chapter Four

HALFWAY TO COLLEGE

Keeping Your Motivation

The altitude in your attitude plays a substantial roll in your child's destiny. If you have few expectations for your child, it will limit his ability to have confidence throughout his K-12 experience. If your attitude is positive, and you have high expectations for your child, it will motivate both of you to do the types of activities that promote your child's success. One of the first steps is to get over any personal fears about college it is an important part of their success. Most children remember to bring this knowledge back to the family. They become an inspiration to your other children. There are many things you can do to maintain a positive attitude. Get over the fear that your child will become more knowledgeable than you. Generally when a child achieves academic success their family sisters, brothers, cousins and sometimes even aunts and uncles have greater aspirations. Write down college admissions questions so that you can get advice from experts in the field.

There are many sources of inspiration that you can read each day. Seek them out in places like the free library and bookstore, in newspapers and magazines or through participation in associations. You can begin to apply positive attitude principles to your own life today. Surround yourself with people who are positive and they will help you have confidence to overcome any of life's challenges. Your attitude is the most important thing you can have. When you expect your child to succeed and go to college, they will aspire to college entrance.

FAST TIPS
- *Use words of encouragement with your child each day.*
- *Continually work on maintaining your own positive attitude.*

HALFWAY TO COLLEGE

Elementary School Learning Strategy

The early years of a child's development establish the foundation for learning. It is important for parents to be fully involved in their child's education. This involvement begins at home by creating a good learning environment. Read books and attend scholastic events with your children. Visit the library. Read to your child in the early years and read with your child when he starts kindergarten. (Full involvement also means you know your child's teachers, volunteer at his school and attend meetings and events.) Another learning resource for young children is books on tapes. These can be borrowed from the library or purchased at the local bookstore. They are fun to listen to and help your child to learn how to read.

If your child is having difficulty in reading, writing or mathematics, seek help at the school level and also in your community. Check with your local community center, library or legislative office. The goal is to continue to provide the highest education for your son or daughter. The early years offer you a tremendous opportunity to help your son or daughter excel academically.

FAST TIPS
- *Seek educational resources for your student.*
- *Read to your son or daughter for at least an hour each day*

Middle School Adjustments

Middle school students face tremendous personal, emotional and social changes. First, they are in a new school environment where they must meet and make new friends. As they enter young adulthood they are establishing their own identity as a person.   They also go through a lot of physical changes and are required to make adjustments toward each other. At the same time, they are also affected by their own hormones. During this stage of life parents must be good listeners. You must pay more attention to your teenager and his friends. Invite his friends to your home so you can get a sense of their goals and direction. A summer barbeque is always a good way to create a relaxing environment where young people can talk freely.

HALFWAY TO COLLEGE

Encourage your middle school student to get involved in school activities, like student government, community service or the school play. Establishing a connection with the school will increase your child's motivation to learn. This will also enable him to have peers who are making positive contributions to the school and community.

Middle school students will begin to develop leadership skills, which will be helpful when they enter high school. Middle school students will pay a lot of attention to things that do not make sense to their parents. One moment they want to be grown up and the next they want to be children.

This is part of moving toward adulthood. During this time in a teenager's life, parents should not expect everyday to be the same. You must be supportive, but firm in reminding your son or daughter of what is right and wrong.

Take your teenager to events where he can learn about new things that he can discuss while at school. Ask teachers for suggestions. There are events that help the learning process become more alive for some students. You can expect some resistance at first, but continue to find different events. You'll be surprised when your son or daughter shows their appreciation.

FAST TIPS
- *Be prepared to listen to younger teenagers when they are having problems in school or in the neighborhood.*
- *Recognize that every child adjusts differently to their middle school.*

Notes

Middle School Identity

Since middle school is a time of physical and emotional changes, parents can play an important role. The physical change that a middle school student is experiencing can heavily affect their motivation on any given day. Parents must take time to understand their child's issues and concerns. Give your young person an opportunity to process some of their own problems and to consider some of the possible solutions.

One moment a student can be very immature and the next moment they can be very sincere. It is all a part of this growing period. It's important to understand the expectations of the school and the teachers who have daily interaction with your student. Meeting with teachers can reaffirm some of the behaviors you've been observing. You and the teacher can work together to build your student's confidence. Parents must also exercise some flexibility. A flexible mindset can help relieve some of the stress that you may experience when you attempt to engage in a conversation with your teenager. Whenever possible try to create opportunities to be one-on-one with your teenager. Listen without judgment to what they are saying. Then ask them why they feel the way they do. Sometimes it is better to offer solutions later rather than advice right away.

FAST TIPS
- *Communicate with your son's or daughter's teacher during the middle school years.*
- *Listen to your son or daughter without judgment so one-on-one communication improves.*

Notes

Chapter Four

HALFWAY TO COLLEGE

Peer Pressure

The emotional pressure your student experiences during high school is much greater than middle school. Don't discount the influence of friends who are a part of your student's life. Friends and other students can be a positive influence or negative influence. Try to encourage your son or daughter and his or her peers to become involved in a youth organization that promotes leadership and positive personal development. Without the positive influence of other students and adults, a young person can easily fall into the wrong crowd. Remind your teenager of your expectations and standards. The seeds that you plant will cause your student to make better choices throughout their lives. Let them know that they are not alone and that there is more than one option when they are feeling negative pressure.

High School Learning Strategy

Ninth grade is not the time for parents to drop out of the educational scene. Your teenager needs you now more then ever. Each year in the United States fifty percent of high school students drop out of school after ninth grade. One major factor is lack of parental involvement during this critical time in their lives. You can start by attending an orientation at your child's school. Also, arrange a meeting with the principal to determine how the school is organized and how your student can meet his teacher's expectations. If you are clear on you student's goals, it will help you to know how to assist them. Your active involvement with the school will help you be aware of your son or daughter's progress and any academic support he or she may need.

Realize that the teachers in a high school have different levels of expectation regarding a student's progress. From the mid-term progress report you will get an idea of your child's successes and challenges. Encourage your child to become involved in school activities, which will become very important when they apply to colleges or trade schools. The admissions officers at most colleges want to know that your child has made connections. These experiences are part of the socialization process that they will continue to encounter as adults. Discuss activities so you can find ways to be supportive. For example, maybe he has decided to run for a school office, you can offer to read over the campaign speech or help make posters. If your child is involved in the school play you could help with stage design, ticket sales or even act as a coach on the day of the event. Of course it may make your teenager feel a bit awkward, but it is an important part of parenting. It is one of those things your child will remember as he thinks about his high school experience. There is also a lot of information you can obtain by doing things at your child's school. Every year you should attend college fairs with your son or daughter.

Gathering scholarship information is something you and your teenager can do year-round. Purchase a binder that you will use to keep all scholarship information together. Use a page in the binder to create a list of deadlines for scholarship applications.

FAST TIPS
- *Encourage your student to get to know their teachers by participating in student government.*
- *Start a scholarship binder that you will use during senior year.*

Notes

HALFWAY TO COLLEGE

How to Expand Your Teenagers Mind

As a teenager your child must not only develop a new ability to memorize more information, they must understand how to learn. Learning is not limited to a teacher's instruction and the corresponding textbook. More information is necessary to strengthen writing and math skills, which will expand learning in all subject areas. When you meet with your teenager's teachers ask about resources they may be using to supplement class instruction. These might include other books, websites, compact discs, DVDs and audiotapes. Making additional resources available can also raise your student's interest level in a subject because the potential for success will improve.

Help Your Student Communicate

Think about how you communicate with your teenager right know. How often do you listen to their perspective so that they know that they can talk with you freely? What is their body language saying about the comfort he or she feels when communicating goals and desires to you? Ask him if he feels that you treat him like he is still in elementary school. Some times it is difficult for parents to make the separation from the early years where guidance was required all the time to the high school years where listening is often enough. Remember a teenager is attempting to form his own personality. Your words can have the power to yield a positive or a negative response from your son or daughter. Ask your child to discuss his biggest communication challenges. Be available and visible during school and sporting events that are important to your child. Show up at his friend's event when you are invited. Your participation will give you greater acceptance with your son's or daughter's peer group.

FAST TIPS
- *Conduct a personal assessment of your communication with your teenager.*
- *Create more opportunities for quality time to talk to your teenager.*

HALFWAY TO COLLEGE

Talking to Other Parents

When raising teenagers it is good to form alliances with other parents. It will help you to balance your conversations with your teenager. This is an important aspect of keeping your communication open. Each generation of teenagers has different pressures that affect their daily lives. Spend time talking to other adult men and women. Each may give you a different perspective of how to handle issues that face your children. You should also consult other parents regarding educational activities that have benefited their teenagers. There are after school programs, volunteer organizations and youth groups that promote the importance of self-image. The amount of time that you invest in networking with parents can relieve your stress and increase your overall knowledge of some of the best practices for investing in your teenager's growth. It will open your mind to some of the influences in education and technology that are affecting your son's or daughter's attitude.

Halfway to College Application

The K-12 years can be some of the most rewarding for you and your child. You have an opportunity to lay the foundation for your student's success. You can help your student by keeping communication open, especially as he transitions from elementary school to middle school and from middle school to high school. Listen to his concerns no matter how large or small. Write down some of the challenges you need to discuss with your son or daughter.

_____

_____

_____

_____

HALFWAY TO COLLEGE

Continue to discuss the issues in a low-pressure environment. Stay in contact with teachers who can help your student make successful adjustments. Reading is a fundamental skill at every age. Every student should read at least an hour each day. Consider purchasing a book series that your student enjoys. Students can become acquainted with a specific author's writing style. For a young child an additional enhancement is listening to books on tape. The child can easily read their book as the tape plays.

Your student should have a book to read at all times. Your student can read more when he has less homework.

Create a list of new books your student will read:

_____

_____

_____

_____

A good learning environment is important when your son or daughter is reading. The quiet environment of a library may be a good alternative. Also consider visiting a bookstore. Many bookstores have areas for small children and adults to read.

List stores and libraries you will visit.

_____

_____

_____

_____

One of the most significant factors for success in college is a student's math skills level. Take the opportunity to talk about math with your child. Ask him to guess the weight of a can of corn or encourage him to estimate the number of inches in a cereal box. Take your child to purchase a sale item. Ask him to figure out how much the 10 percent discount is on the clothing item you are purchasing.

HALFWAY TO COLLEGE

List potential math learning opportunities.

_____

_____

_____

_____

Help your student to get a better understanding of the cost of living. Use play money and let your student pay for his own living expenses for a week. Include utilities, clothes, food, transportation and other items. Give your student a paycheck amount then ask them to deduct or pay for the resources they are using in your home.

Make a list of bills your student will pay:

_____

_____

_____

_____

Remember that there are companies that produce software for K12 students. Most students will benefit from interactive software programs.

Notes

HALFWAY TO COLLEGE

What Parents Are Saying
Kelly Woodland

1.   It's important to create a quiet and distraction free environment.

2.   Read a variety of books every month. Always encourage your child to have a book they can read when they are in the car or when you are visiting a friend.

3.   Get your son/daughter to create a clutter free place to study.

4.   Send your child to a special academic camp over the summer. (i.e computer, math, science exploration).

5.   Encourage your child to look at study time as a form of practice similar to that of track, basketball or football. They must commit to working on their mental strength.

6.   Identify a mentor who will invest their time in helping your child to make positive career decisions.

7.   Attend regular teacher meetings that are scheduled to occur during the year.

8.   Make sure that you are actively involved with your student's teacher when your child makes the transition from elementary to middle school and from middle school to high school.

9.   Don't be afraid to ask your son/daughter's teacher about tutoring if they are maintaining low grades on examinations.

Making it to College

1.   Develop a network with different types of families whose children have attended college.

2.   Start the habit of reading articles in the newspaper and on the internet about college life.

3. Remember a students level of math skills is the most significant indicator of a students potential of college graduation. Encourage your student to take courses beyond Algebra II.

4. Talk to several college admissions officers about the requirement to get your child admitted.

5. Visit the library regularly to find out about new services they are offering.

6. Send your teenage student to a PSAT or SAT course.

7. Agree with your child on a list of seven colleges that are top on their application list.

8. Take your child to museums and theater so that they can have an appreciation for the arts.

9. Don't rule out community college if your son/daughter is not ready to attend a four year college.

10. Create a home library that you fill with books such as SAT preparation, college reviews, scholarships and what to take to college.

Halfway to College Activities

1. List the top five local and long distance colleges that your student may want to attend. Plan visits to each of the local colleges.

2. Create a binder that you will fill with scholarship information. Ask about scholarships everywhere you go.

3. Ask a local college student to mentor your student.

4. Encourage your student to become involved with an education organization that has a mission related to college preparation.

HALFWAY TO COLLEGE

Next Steps Worksheet

What have you learned?

_____
_____
_____
_____
_____
_____
_____
_____
_____
_____

How will you apply this information?

_____
_____
_____
_____
_____
_____
_____
_____
_____
_____

What is the first step that you will take?

_____
_____
_____
_____
_____
_____
_____

Chapter Four

HALFWAY TO COLLEGE

Next Steps Worksheet

How will you use this information to help your son/daughter?

_____

_____

_____

_____

_____

_____

_____

_____

_____

_____

_____

GET TO KNOW THE TEACHER

Understanding the Parent and Teacher Relationship

Parents frequently skip Parent Teacher Night thinking it is just another meeting. For parents who want their son or daughter to succeed, it is not just another meeting. It is a valuable opportunity to talk with teachers. One of the most important information gathering opportunities of the year is a meeting with your student's teacher. The teacher spends a considerable amount of time each week with your student in their class. Teachers continually assess motivation and learning capabilities of students during class discussions, quizzes, and tests. They gather important information about students that parents never see at home. When you don't attend the Parent Teacher meeting at your child's school, it sends a message that you are not concerned.

How can you and your student benefit from the information that you gather at the meeting? If your student is succeeding, you can discuss more ways to increase his learning opportunities. There may be after school programs, student organizations or tutoring that a teacher or counselor will share in a one-on-one meeting. If your son or daughter is facing challenges in a class, the teacher may suggest sources of help your student has not mentioned.

Some students are not mature enough to know that the investment of additional time will actually improve their grades. You can get to know certain teachers by volunteering on school-organized projects, like community senior citizen events, school trips, school plays, or sporting events. You want to build a reputation for being involved and concerned about what is happening. It is never too late during the school year to get involved. Make yourself known. You will reap the benefit through contact with the teachers who will share their information even more easily then in a one-on-one meetings.

FAST TIPS
- *Meet all of your student's teachers at Parent Teacher Night.*
- *Volunteer for special projects so that you can get to know other teachers.*

GET TO KNOW THE TEACHER

Uncover the best Pre-College Programs

There are more than 100 programs geared toward college preparation in cities across the country. Your investigation should start at the main school district office in your city. Contact the main office and ask them if they offer pre-college programs at different levels - for elementary, middle or high school. Be specific with your request.

If they do not have a central office, call local schools and inquire about their programs. Some occur during school hours and others occur after school. Some may be offered on Saturdays over a series of weeks. Sometimes involvement in these programs is all that a student needs to focus their talents and prepare for college.

 It is never too early to let your son or daughter visit a college campus. A visit to a college campus helps take away the anxiety and fear that can come when a student is new to the college environment. There are college tours that organizations provide for a minimal fee. These tours often cover several states. You might start at Temple University in Philadelphia and end up at Florida A & M University five days later.

Here is a list of summer programs that I have found helpful to parents. I am familiar with these programs, but you should not limit yourself to just these. There are programs that help like gifted programs, Upward Bound, Talent Search, Inroads, Mesa, pre-college centers located on college campuses, Community and Schools, and College Access.

FAST TIPS
- *Middle school and high school is the time to pursue pre-college programs.*
- *Visit college campuses so that you and your student can assess strengths and weaknesses.*

GET TO KNOW THE TEACHER

Parent Teacher Association

All schools should have a Parent Teacher Association. The purpose of the Parent Teacher Association is to give parents a voice in the decisions and policies that affect their children. Opinions about the school, its facility and teaching practices are given and heard because of the number of people who are involved in the Association. The Parent Teacher Association's also raise funds for important school projects. Some school districts have a central Parent Teacher Association (PTA), which gathers information from all the parents who are around the city.

It also provides additional information to the local PTA and serves as a representative for all the needs that all the parents may have. Some central associations provide resources that are often available in a community center setting, but are unique to the school district. The PTA can request additional tutoring for students, after school programs, and support for teachers. It requires a team effort to make an Association work. Parents who are involved should encourage participation from parents who are inactive. The Parent Teacher Association is a valuable resource for any parent. You can find out about scholarships, grants, special programs, and even private schools of interest.

FAST TIPS
- *The Parent Teacher Association acts as an advocate for your student.*
- *The Parent Teacher Association offers special programs and scholarships.*

Notes

GET TO KNOW THE TEACHER

Attending a Community College

Every parent should maximize the amount of information their student can learn before entering a four-year college. One way to expose your son or daughter to college life is by enrolling them in community college while they are still in high school. Some schools do not offer certain courses so students take them at the local community college. For example, some advanced math classes may not be available at the high school level. For a student who is interested in engineering, science or mathematics, these courses are critical and can provide the appropriate challenge. If the school district doesn't pay for such college courses ask if you can pay for the course yourself. Some parents have also enrolled their high school students in summer courses. So some students have enough credits to begin college during the second semester of their freshman year. This early exposure to higher learning gives students even more confidence.

FAST TIPS
- *Ask your son or daughter's school if community college courses are available.*
- *Let your student know that they will need to study at least three hours a day.*

Choosing a High School

Selecting a high school is an easy process if you start early. Start while your son or daughter is in seventh grade. Get in touch with the Parent Teacher Association of the school you are considering and talk with parents whose children attend the school. Ask about the curriculum so you can determine the type of classes offered. Schools that offer advance level classes in a high school are schools that are considered highly academic. As I mentioned, if you favor a particular school that does not offer advanced classes, consider community college. Set up a meeting with the school counselor to discuss how many students attend college or trade school. Find out what kind of assistance they will provide for a student who is considering college. Ask if students from their school have won scholarships to attend college. Ask if they have a college prep program that your son or daughter can begin in ninth grade. Don't miss the date to submit your school district's paperwork. Waiting on you student to get the form may not be the best approach. Call the school district office so that you can get the form directly and mail it in on time. This will ensure that you are selecting the best high school for your son or daughter.

GET TO KNOW THE TEACHER

Knowing Your Student's Teacher Application

1. Try to find different types of educational experiences for your child. This exposure can help a child to uncover his gifts and talents. For example take your child to a local theater or a high school play, visit an aquarium or participate in a painting lesson at a museum. Try to visit a science center on a college campus or in your community. Children of all ages love to participate in scientific experiments or competitions. Look in your local newspaper or on the Internet for events in your neighborhood.

List different types of events your son or daughter should attend.

_____

_____

_____

2. It's never too early to start thinking about the best middle school or high school for your child. Arrange a visit so that you can see how the schools are organized. Also take your student to visit a few local colleges and speak with college students when they are in middle and high school. There may be a special college preparation program that your student can attend.

FAST TIPS
- *Begin researching high schools when your child is in seventh grade.*
- *Submit high school admissions forms on time.*

Notes

GET TO KNOW THE TEACHER

Make a list of places you will visit throughout the school year.

_____

_____

_____

_____

3. Talk with your student about their goals. Sit down and create an outline of the types of cultural and academic exposure your student needs. Talk with his teacher about creative learning opportunities.

4. Actively participate in the school your son or daughter attends. The teachers will get to know you and they will share their insights about your child. Your child's teacher will also know that you are ready to help your child in any way possible.

5. Always look for an opportunity to give your student exposure to additional educational opportunities. Special advanced courses may challenge your high school student. Advanced class instructors do a great job of preparing students for college. If an advanced course gets too challenging ask your child's teacher about tutoring.

Create a list of challenging courses that your student take:

_____

_____

_____

_____

6. Today, educational opportunities are available in the United States and abroad. Consider allowing your child to visit another country. A visit to another country can be especially helpful when a student is studying a foreign language. This experience will also help improve your child's ability to function in a changing global society.

Chapter Five

GET TO KNOW THE TEACHER

Dr. Keith and Mrs. Monika Moo Young

1. Read to your children in the early years and they enjoy reading for a lifetime.
2. Homework should be completed immediately after coming home from school
3. Check their homework daily and make certain that all of it is complete
4. No playing on the computer until their homework is done
5. Go to parent teacher conferences when you are invited to your child's school.
6. Attend field trips with your child it will give you a fun opportunity to communicate with teachers.
7. Ask your child about his day each day
8. Give your child a hug and kiss before he goes to school.
9. Pray with your child before they leave for school.
10. Take your child to church. There are tremendous skills that they can learn.

Teacher Summary

1. Teach your son/daughter the importance of following direction on every test.

2. Maintain good communication with each of your children's teachers.

3. Where possible enroll your son/daughter into advanced courses in math, English and science.

4. Go on trips with the school so that the teachers can get to know you.

5. Ask the teacher about special programs that offer your child new learning experiences.

6. Don't allow the school to set low expectations for your child. Seek tutoring and additional help from local colleges when your child needs help with courses.

7. Ask the teacher about your child's learning style and how you can help them at home.

8. Don't wait for the teacher to send out the grade report. Contact all of them after the first four weeks for a progress report.

9. Ask the teacher what they are doing to prepare students for college.

Knowing your Student's Teacher
Study Activities

1. Meet with all of your student's teachers at the beginning of the school year. Ask them about important test and quiz dates.

2. Ask your child's teachers for a list of books that will help your child better learn the coursework.

3. Make sure that teachers have your telephone number and your e-mail so that they can stay in contact with you.

Notes

GET TO KNOW THE TEACHER

Next Steps Worksheet

What have you learned?

_____

_____

_____

_____

_____

_____

_____

How will you apply this information?

_____

_____

_____

_____

_____

_____

_____

_____

_____

What is the first step that you will take?

_____

_____

_____

_____

_____

Chapter Five

GET TO KNOW THE TEACHER

Next Steps Worksheet

How will you use this information to help your son or daughter?

_____

_____

_____

_____

_____

_____

_____

_____

_____

Chapter Six

CREATE A HOMEWORK STUDY PLAN

Developing a Study Plan

What is a study plan? It is an organized plan that will enable your child to obtain good grades. An effective study plan starts with a time management schedule, which you can begin to use with your son or daughter at any age. It will help your child to become better organized. The schedule should include all classes, study times, tests, quizzes and due dates for projects. Your student needs to know all the resources needed and requirements necessary to succeed in each class. He should write down the dates to start and finish every project. Then organize a list of the materials that he will need. Purchase needed items as soon as possible.

If your student wants to have a successful academic year, the time management schedule must be used effectively. Know dates of all quizzes and tests far in advance. Your child doesn't want to be caught off guard because he isn't prepared. Your student should ask the teacher if there is a schedule he can receive for different types of tests. He should include it as part of his study plan. Test your student prior to an examination or quiz. Friday is generally a big day for testing at most schools. Have your student try to write down all the words that he needs to pronounce if he is having a spelling test. Then practice them with your student. Testing your child can give him confidence and reduce test anxiety for a more successful examination. Your child's study plan should also include activities that motivate him to excel in each class.

Parents must express excitement when their student performs well on a test, quiz or project. All students like to be rewarded for their accomplishments. Your words have a powerful influence on your child's motivation to succeed. Place your son or daughter's special awards on the kitchen refrigerator or on the bedroom door. Honor your child with a special day when he's overcome

Chapter Six

an obstacle in a class that is difficult. Take him out for dinner or just take him out for fun. Tell other family members like grandparents, uncles and aunts so that they can also reward your child for an accomplishment. Give teachers positive feedback when they provide personal assistance to your son or daughter. If a teacher knows that you are sincerely interested in your child's success they will be supportive.

FAST TIPS
- *Acknowledge teachers when they provide special support for your student.*
- *Review a list of key words that will be on your student's next examination.*

Map Your Student's Education

Every student has unique characteristics. The question that a parent must ask is, "How do I understand these characteristics and use this information to map my child's education?" The word mapping will help you to focus on a specific direction to follow. There are many roads that you can take, but you must choose the best one for your child. It is clear to me that the road for each individual child can be different based on their unique characteristics and how they respond to the world around them. Specific events and memories can affect how a child responds in a particular situation. If your student has a bad experience with a teacher then he may believe that all teachers are against him. For another child this teacher may force him to work harder. This child has a different view of the world and a different attitude about his abilities. Parents should be careful not to show favoritism. Just because one child responds like you would, and the other is shy, do not limit his potential. A lot of introverted children grow up to be exceptional people who effectively change the world around them.

FAST TIPS
- *Have your child make a list of his individual strengths and challenges. Help him or her overcome their challenges.*
- *Encourage your child to continually prepare for examinations and quizzes.*

CREATE A HOMEWORK STUDY PLAN

Learning How to Learn

When a child is a baby he learns how to explore his environment. He learns to conduct his own experiments to see how things work. Just as children explore together to obtain new information, adults often intervene because they foresee some of the dangers in a child's play. Part of helping a child grow is letting them go.

Teaching your student how to learn includes exposing him to different types of learning environments. Every student is trying to figure out the value of the information he receives from teachers, peers, and parents. One teacher may present information that is new and exciting, while another teacher focuses on the basics. As you listen to your student talk about the new things he is exploring, maintain your enthusiasm throughout the conversation. A student who is ready to learn will pursue every opportunity to gain new knowledge. A parent's objective is to create a home environment where your student can experiment. Your student may learn well from interactive computer games or by attending plays at a local theater.

FAST TIPS
- *Purchase games and experiments you and your student can use at home.*
- *Consider purchasing interactive math computer software.*

Learning From Your Teacher

A parent can learn a lot from becoming an extension of the school environment in the home. You can be certain that the teachers who instruct your student today are using totally different methods. They may even have different resources to teach subjects like English and math. On more than one occasion my 9-year-old daughter has demonstrated a new method for answering a math problem. The teacher should be your resource when there is a subject you do not understand. Make sure that you have a telephone number and an e-mail to communicate with your child's instructor. Get the help that your student needs right away. Be persistent. The squeaky wheel gets the oil.

CREATE A HOMEWORK STUDY PLAN

One of the most frequent complaints you will hear from your student is that he does not understand his teacher. Spend time discussing this topic with your student. There are three possible issues: (1) your student does not understand the subject, (2) the teacher teaches too fast for your student to comprehend the subject or (3) the instructor's teaching style does not match up with the way that your student learns. Once you have uncovered the source of the classroom challenge begin to pursue solutions. Talk with the teacher, obtain your student's textbook, locate a DVD he can study, obtain a tutor from a local college or meet with the Dean to get additional resources.

Your goal is to make the teacher an advocate for your student. Teachers can appreciate when parents make an effort to increase their child's learning potential. Give positive reinforcementon a subject where your student is already having success. Whenever possible try to demonstrate how learning one subject well can improve his performance in another. For example, writing well can influence your son's or daughter's grades when taking a history examination. The relationship you form with your child's teacher can greatly enhance the schooling you do at home. You will have a student who is more prepared for difficult subjects. Your student will also know how he can independently obtain the help he needs in any class.

FAST TIPS

- *Try to have quarterly meetings with your student's teacher.*
- *Reward your student when he consistently makes good grades.*

Notes

CREATE A HOMEWORK STUDY PLAN

Why Students Must Complete Projects

Throughout K-12 and college your student will receive assignments to complete various projects. The best method for success is for students to choose topics that interest them. Students who select their own topics are more likely to invest the energy necessary to present a successful project. Be prepared to find the materials that motivate your student to complete their project early. Students who start late limit the quality of their project. Most instructors can identify a carefully designed project.

Project work provides a student with the type of experience he needs when working for a company. Once your student has decided on a project topic he will need to establish a timeline to follow. There should be major markers in his personal calendar to let him assess his progress. Encourage your student to seek input from his instructor to save time and effort in terms of any adjustments that may be needed at the last minute. Your son or daughter may also arrange an assessment of the project from another teacher. If your student keeps an open mind, they can successfully design a project that receives the best grade in the class.

FAST TIPS
- *Map out a few of the local libraries your student will visit.*
- *Pick up dictionaries and check the internet for tutors.*

The Library Is Still an Outstanding Resource

Many students think that a library is a thing of the past. They say that computers offer a tremendous amount of information that they can access right away. They would rather search the Internet from the convenience of their home. The library is still a great place to gather information and to learn about a variety of topics. If you have a student who really likes to read, the library is a free source of books. When you encourage reading you are laying the foundation for your student's success in K-12 and college.

Chapter Six

CREATE A HOMEWORK STUDY PLAN

The library offers several resources, like books on tape, DVDs, CDs, video tapes and even lectures by experts in the community. These experts could be teachers, college professors or writers who will read passages from their books. Your students may enjoy hearing this type of oral presentation.

You may want to talk to the librarian about the topic your student is researching. Some librarians work in special sections of the library and can provide your student with in-depth information about a certain topic. Talking to a specific librarian can save time.

Many teachers and professors still require students to use certain book references for term papers. Your student should keep his information options open and consider visiting a community college or university library.

Creating A Homework Study Plan Application

1. A vital aspect of every teacher's instruction is the assignment of homework. Homework is given to students to reinforce the lecture notes. A student should be able to derive two benefits from completing assignments. The first benefit is that reading assignments and math scores improve when homework is completed on time. To stay on schedule all homework should be handed in on time from the very first week of school. Second, completing assignments will help students to form good study habits for college and beyond.

Create a list of all projects that are due.

Start
Date_____Project_____

Start
Date_____Project_____

Start
Date_____Project_____

Start
Date_____Project_____

CREATE A HOMEWORK STUDY PLAN

2. A student may not have homework every night, but he should still seek learning opportunities. Your student should get into the habit of reading course-related books on his own time. He should always have an extra book that he is reading for fun.

3. Create a positive learning environment in your home. Your child can only study well if there is adequate lighting and a desk full of good study resources. The desk and area where your student frequently studies should also provide reinforcement for his many academic successes. Hang up highly graded papers and certificates in this area.

Develop a place in your home where your student can study.

_____

_____

_____

4. Creating an academic plan will help your student feel more organized. Tell your student to practice the habit of organizing his notes immediately after the school day is over. This may reveal something that he didn't write down. Maximize his participation in the learning process by knowing the types of materials your child will need to improve learning in each course.

5. The quality of your son's or daughter's homework can affect his or her overall grade. Your child should be sure to review all answers for accuracy. A written document should be reviewed by an adult. Remember, the writer of a document can not always see his mistakes.

Who are the people you will ask to review your students papers?

_____

_____

_____

_____

Chapter Six

CREATE A HOMEWORK STUDY PLAN

6. Students should complete all written assignments on a computer. There are three main benefits. The first is that the student can easily make changes. Second, spell-check can review documents for errors and allows your student to make corrections. Third, a grammar-check will offer alternative sentence structure. Most students use Microsoft Word to complete their documents.

7. Your student may occasionally want to use a computer program called Excel to help showcase or validate data to be included in a paper or project. Excel is good software program that you may use to create financial reports.

8. One way to strengthen your student's ability to do homework is to have him complete more homework than assigned. If your student has completed all of his math homework, he should look for additional problems in another book. A student should never think that the assigned textbook is the only book he can read. Visit the library or a bookstore to find additional resources.

Create a list of additional books your son or daughter can use.

_____

_____

_____

_____

9. Throughout K-12 your student will receive assignments to complete. He may create environmental posters or a cell membrane made out of clay. Your student should start all homework projects a month or two before they are due. Starting early will give your student the flexibility to complete all his homework on time.

CREATE A HOMEWORK STUDY PLAN

What Parents are Saying
Rita and Alphonso Scarborough

1. Limit the hours your son/daughter watches television each week. Our limits are one hour during the week and 4-6 hours on the weekend.

2. Require all homework to be completed daily before your son/daughter is allowed to spend time on the internet or gameboy.

3. Create your own weekly quizzes and tests on the materials in your students notebook.

4. Allow homework to be done in an area of the house that is relaxing.

5. Get in the habit of posting new terms, concepts, etc on the important study locations around your home.

6. Ask your students teacher for a mid-term progress report.

7. Review terms you do not understand in a dictionary or on the internet.

8. Get plenty of sleep the night before all examinations and quizzes.

9. Have great expectations of what your child can accomplish.

10. Shower your child with praise when they have a fantastic grade on a test or project.

Create a Homework Study Plan Summary

1. Homework should not be the last thing a student does when they come home from school. They should start their study time at home right away.

2. Keep binders of previous home work assignments so your student can always refer to information from their notes.

3. Post good home work grades on the refrigerator and on your child's desk.

4. Enter your child into art and science contest that are offered at school and in the community.

5. Volunteer to tutor other students so that you will have great success in school.

6. Projects that your son/daughter complete must be reviewed early.

7. Review the end of your chapter for questions that your student can answer.

8. Use the early years which are K-4 grades to establish a good reading foundation.

9. Look on the internet for homework that other schools are assigning.

10. Continue to increase the size of your effort to make sure that all homework is delivered to the teacher.

Study Plan Activities

1. In a small groups of parents, develop a list of 20 positive at-home learning strategies. Share your list with your entire group.

2. Develop a study plan for how you would prepare your son or daughter for two examinations on the same day.

3. Develop your student's own report card listing current courses and grades. Discuss strategies to improve your student's grades.

4. Create a list of your student's long-term goals for the next two years. Discuss how he can avoid obstacles that may prevent him from accomplishing his goal.

Notes

CREATE A HOMEWORK STUDY PLAN

Next Steps Worksheet

What have you learned?

_____
_____
_____
_____
_____
_____
_____

How will you apply this information?

_____
_____
_____
_____
_____
_____
_____

What is the first step that you will take?

_____
_____
_____
_____
_____

How will you use this information to help your son or daughter?

_____
_____
_____
_____
_____
_____

COLLEGE 101

Getting Over Your Fear

Sometimes it is not the student's fears, but the parent's fears, about college that can be overwhelming. It can be especially difficult for a parent who is sending their first child off to college. There is a great fear of the unknown, especially with regard to the health and safety of your child. There may also be fears about how your student will succeed in the classroom. Communication with your student is the best way to get over your fears. Don't bottle up all of your feelings. Talk to a friend who has a successful student enrolled in college. Share some of your fears and ask for advice. You will discover that you are going through some of the same emotions that other parents have when they sent their first student to college.

Why Attend Orientation?

Attending orientation is one of the most effective ways for parents to alleviate their anxieties. Most orientation programs occur during the summer so that parents can feel free to take a vacation day for the visit. During orientation colleges showcase faculty and resources. Some colleges even invite parents to stay in the student residences to get a sense of what college life will be like for their children. You can also find out more about the curriculum and ask questions of the faculty. Students will also be on hand to talk about activities and student organizations. I encourage you to ask your student to participate in least one campus organization. Take a full tour of the campus and ask for business cards so that you can keep in touch periodically.

What Your Student Should Take to College

Some students pull up to their college dorm with a truck load of things from home, only to discover that the room they will be staying in is not large enough to accommodate all of their things. It's far better to create a list of things to bring before you go. My recommendation is that you focus on the essential items that every college student needs. These include toiletries, blankets, a lamp, a computer, clothes and shoes, writing supplies and books. If you meet your child's roommate early you may discover that only one television is necessary.

You can call the residence hall office to inquire about the size of your student's bed. Bring a pillow that he is familiar with. A little touch of home may make it easier to make the transition. Also, bring a top cover and a blanket to fit the bed. Some colleges will allow a small refrigerator in the room, but ask first. There may be a community microwave that everyone on the floor uses. Most colleges do not allow hot plates because they are considered fire hazards.

Purchasing Educational Resources

It is important that you provide the resources that a student needs to excel in each class in college. The first thing that you should do is purchase a file cabinet to keep all your student's information organized. The cabinet should have drawers and hanging files. In the first drawer, pencils, ink pens, erasers, protractors and other instruments can be stored. The second drawer should have loose-leaf paper, typing paper and resume paper neatly organized. College instructors expect to receive typed home work assignments. Glue, staples, staplers, correcting fluid, paper clips, tacks, tape and other resources should be available. Sometimes it is cheaper to buy these items in bulk when they are on sale. Take advantage of special offers that maybe announced in the local newspapers.

Go to an arts and crafts store to buy supplies for special projects. It is important for your student to have these materials on hand so that he is not running around the night before a project is due. Teachers are always looking for exceptional efforts on projects and they will reward students for their efforts.

Every student should have a library card so they can access a local or larger library. Your student should also have a dictionary, a thesaurus, a dictionary of synonyms, a dictionary of antonyms, and a rhyming dictionary. You should also purchase specialty dictionaries such as computer dictionaries, grammar dictionaries, science dictionaries, foreign language dictionaries, and encyclopedia. There are also several college preparation websites where this type of information can be found. Having his or her own library will help your student to understand the importance of researching information.

FAST TIPS

- *After each study session students should ask themselves what they have learned. Encourage students to write notes of important points while they study.*

How To Submit Projects and Term Papers on Time

Every parent knows his child's strengths and weaknesses. One area that is a consistent challenge for parents is getting their students to submit their projects and term papers on time. Students do not start projects on time because they have an unrealistic sense of the amount of time required to complete the project and anxiety of how to get started. Some students are so anxious that they wait until the last minute, which results in lower grades. The parent's role is to be aware of these pitfalls. Help your son or daughter to get started. The first step is to have your son or daughter use a calendar to write down start dates for each project. Each project should have a weekly goal, like the collection of materials, picking of books from library and the typing that is required for the term paper itself. If it is a project that will be displayed, the first week should be spent gathering the raw materials required. The key to success is organizational planning. If your student is writing a term paper, the first week should be focused on determining the main topics and developing an outline. If the student is having difficulty selecting a topic then ask friends or family for help.

College 101 Application

Preparation for college can be a positive life-changing experience. To help alleviate stress discuss the progress your student is making with the completion of each application. Help your student to identify people who can give him a good recommendation.

COLLEGE 101

1. Write down all of the important people who can provide your child with a recommendation letter for college. Remember they will need sufficient time to write one.

Contact_____

Contact_____

Contact_____

Contact_____

Contact_____

2. Review all of the documentation your student needs for college admission.
3. Organize a schedule so that you can spend special one-on-one time with your student.

> **Develop a list of places that you would like to visit with your college-bound student. Senior year is a special time when you need to create times to talk with your student.**

Create a list of activities.

Activities_____

Activities_____

Activities_____

Activities_____

Activities_____

4. During January begin to discuss the types of items your student will need for college.

> **Try to purchase these items on sale.**

Create a list of these items.

Shopping Items_____

Shopping Items_____

Shopping Items_____

Shopping Items_____

The money you save when purchasing these items can be used to pay for college textbooks.

5. Always think of academic resources that can help your student to prepare for college. Get your student into the habit of seeking out a tutor whenever he needs help.

6. Encourage your student to meet with his teachers to get help. This is an important strategy for college. When your student meets with a college faculty member he raises his chances of learning additional information that can help him in class.

7. You may want to have a discussion about your student's learning style. Your student should get into a habit of creating unique ways to understand textbook materials. You can also help your student to understand how to make adjustments when a teacher is difficult.

Ask your student to describe the teaching style they prefer.

List these teaching techniques.
Key Teaching Techniques

1._____
2._____
3._____
4._____

8. Be an important resource to your child. Remind him that class attendance will be an important part of his success. Some instructors will include class participation in a student's grade.

9. Remind your student that he will determine his own grade based on effort. Each student must maximize the amount of time spent studying. Your student can benefit from knowing the grade he can expect to receive based on his commitment to meet teachers and to obtain tutoring when needed.

COLLEGE 101

What Are Parents Saying

Dr. Doreen Loury, Arcadia University

1. Earning a college degree must be a part of the family culture.

2. Discuss the value of a college education in terms of career opportunities.

3. Make your child aware that there are a variety of public and private institutions. There are 4 year colleges, 2 year colleges, trade schools, business schools and special training schools (i.e. computer, flight schools, scuba diving)

4. There are different types of degrees such as associates, bachelors, masters and doctorate.

5. Tutoring must be viewed as an asset not a crutch because your son/daughter is having difficulties.

6. Set up a standard for excellence in terms of the types of grades your child is expected to earn.

7. Establish a standard of excellence in your son/daughters personal, spiritual and emotional life.

8. Parents must be advocates for their child's education needs. Stay connected with teachers and counselors at your son/daughters high school. Discuss the schools role in preparing students for college.

Notes

COLLEGE 101

College 101 Summary

1.   Visit colleges beginning with the ninth grade.

2.   It's important for students to have good grades from 9th thru 12th grade.

3.   Don't pay attention to friends who discourage you from sending your child to college.

4.   Meet with the school counselor and talk about colleges that their students attend.

5.   Gather an extensive list of college scholarships. Put the scholarships into categories in a binder.

6.   Attend a variety of college fairs and fill out forms to get on colleges mailing list.

7.   Find ways to talk to the college students who have attended the college your son/daughter is visiting.

8.   Keep a positive attitude about your son/daughters acceptance to college.

9.   Tell your student to join an organization so that they will have a good list of extra-curricular activities to list on college applications.

10.   Enroll your student in national organizations that teach leadership skills. Colleges look for students with leadership skills.

Notes

COLLEGE 101

College 101 Activities

1. Organize a list of books your student will need for college.

2. Get together with some of your student's friends and create a list of questions they have about college.

3. Schedule a time to meet with your student's school counselor to find out about college preparatory programs.

4. Conduct Internet research on colleges of interest. Ask your student to ask his teachers if they know anyone who has attended these schools or if they can suggest other colleges or universities.

Notes

Next Steps Worksheet

What have you learned?

_____

_____

_____

_____

_____

_____

_____

How will you apply this information?

_____

_____

_____

_____

_____

_____

_____

_____

What is the first step that you will take?

_____

_____

_____

_____

_____

_____

_____

Chapter Seven

How will you use this information to help your son or daughter?

_____

_____

_____

_____

_____

_____

_____

_____

_____

_____

Notes

Chapter Seven

APPENDIX

College Preparation for High School Students

Mathematics (3 to 4 years)

Algebra I
Algebra II
Geometry
Trigonometry
Precalculus
Calculus

English (3 to 4 years)

Composition
American Literature
English Literature
World literature

History & Geography (3 to 4 yrs.)

Geography
U.S. History
U.S. Government
World History
World Culture/Civics

Sciences (2 to 3 years)

Biology
Earth Science
Chemistry
Physics

Language (2 to 3 years)

French
German
Spanish
Japanese
Russian

Arts (2 to 3 years)

Art
Dance
Drama
Music

Electives (1 to 3 years)

Economics or Psychology
Psychology or Statics or Computers

U.S. Dept. of Ed., Preparing Your Child for College, 1996- 97

APPENDIX

Financial Aid/Scholarship Resources

There are many financial resources for students from all income levels. Don't be discouraged by those who say there is no money for your child to attend college.

For current information about federal financial aid, contact the U.S. Department of Education at: 1-800-USA-Learn, or 1-800-4FED-AID.

Pell - Federal grant program for college students sponsored by the United States Department of Education

FSEOG - Federal grant program for college students sponsored by the United States Department of Education

Federal Stafford Loan - These are subsidized and unsubsidized loans for college students.

Federal Plus Loan- This loan provides money that parents can use for their child's education.

State Grants - Most states offers grants for in-state residents. Call your state education department.

Scholarships - Opportunities to obtain scholarships are around you everyday. Some of the places to pursue scholarships are included in the following list:

▪**Family** ▪**Community Groups** ▪**Sororities and Fraternities**

▪**Politicians (i.e. State Representative, Senator, Congressperson)**

▪**Parent's Credit Union or Job** ▪**The Internet**

▪**Local Stores** ▪**Churches**

APPENDIX

Financial Aid Web Sites

- ❖ U.S. Dept of Education:www.ed.gov
- ❖ www.iwc.pair.com/scholarshipage
- ❖ Student Financial Aid Association
- ❖ www. wired scholar.com/usafunds
- ❖ Scholarship Search:www.fastweb.com
- ❖ www. greatgiveaway.salliemae.com
- ❖ Scholarship Search: www.srexpress.com
- ❖ www. college-scholarships.com
- ❖ www. free_scholarship_searches
- ❖ www.finaid.org
- ❖ www.cashe.org
- ❖ www. scholarships-ar-us.org/ moresearches.htm
- ❖ www.fafsa.ed.gov
- ❖ www.cns.gov
- ❖ www.gatesfoundation.org
- ❖ www.gmsp.org
- ❖ www.nsbe.org
- ❖ www.nacme.org
- ❖ www.pheaamentor.org
- ❖ www.bridges.com
- ❖ www.freschinfo.com/index.phtml
- ❖ www.salliemae.com
- ❖ www.ed.gov/prog_info/SFA/1998-9/index.html

APPENDIX

PSAT Books

1. Kaplan PSAT 2006. By: Kaplan

2. Cracking the PSAT 2006 (College Test Prep)
   By: Jeff Rubenstein and Adam Robinson

3. How to Prepare for the PSAT/NMSQT, Barrons How to Prepare for the PSAT/NMSQT Preliminary Scholastic Aptitude Test/National Merit Scholarship Qualifying Examination)
   By: Sharon Weiner Green and Ira.K., Ph.D Wolf

4. Princeton Review PSAT. By Princeton Review

5. Kaplan SAT/ACT/PSAT 2006 Platinum
   By: Windows

6. Peterson PSAT Success
   By: Byron Demmer and Shelley Tarbell

7. McGraw Hill PSAT/NMSQT
   By: Christopher Black and Mark Anestis

8. In a Flash PSAT.
   By: Shirley Tarbell and Cathy Fillmore Hoyt

9. PSAT/NMSQT (REA) The Bbest Study and Coaching course for the PSAT
   By: Suzanne Cofield nd Anita Price Davis

10. Cliffs Test Prep SAT/PSAT 2nd Edition
    Jerry Bobrow

11. Kaplan High Score SAT/ACT/PSAT. By: Kaplan

12. Peterson's PSAT/NMSQT Flash: The Quick Way to Build Math, Verbal, Writing Skills for the new   PSAT/NMSQT and Beyond.
    Shirley Torbell, Cathy Fillmore Hoyt, Peterson's

13. PSAT Exam Cram 2005
    Advantage Education

APPENDIX

SAT Study Books

The Official SAT Study Guide: For The New SAT: College Board.

Up Your Score: The Underground Guide to the SAT: Revised for 2005-2006.
By Larry Berger

11 Practice Test for the SAT and PSAT: With Free Access to the Online
Score Reports and More SAT Help. By Princeton Review

Preparing for the SAT
By: David Horuchi

Gruber's Complete Preparation for the New SAT. 10th Edition
By: Gary Gruber

SAT 2006, Premier Program (Kaplan SAT:Book and CD) By Kaplan

Cracking the New SAT 2006 (College Test Prep).
By: Adam Robinson

McGRaw Hill SAT I
By: Christopher Block

The Rocket Review Revolution: The Ultimate Guide to The New SAT
By: Adam Robinson

Math Workbook for the New SAT. (Barron's Workbook for the SAT I)
By: Lawrence Leff

Verbal Workbook for the New SAT. (Barron's Workbook for the SAT I)
By: Sharon Weiner Green

Kaplan New SAT Writing Workbook
By: Kaplan

Kaplan New SAT Reading Workbook
By: Kaplan

Peterson:New SAT Writing Workbook: (Academic Test Preparation series.
By: Margaret Moram

College Planning Guide

The first two years of high school lay the foundation for the junior and senior years. The school coaches, faculty, staff, and students should help to make each year count by focusing on academic excellence and pre-college preparation planning steps.

9TH AND 10TH GRADE CHECK LIST

- Checklist

- Buy a calendar or daily planner and use it to remember to complete class assignments and after-school activities

- Read all types of books in addition to books assigned by your teachers

- Explore different careers by talking with people who work in that field or your counselor

- Create a college folder to keep all college related materials.

- Visit colleges when you have an opportunity

Notes

11th Grade Check List

September

- Buy another calendar which you will use to keep track of important assignments

- Buy another folder to keep all of your college materials

- Take the PSAT and enroll in a SAT prep course at a local university or school

- Stay involved in sports and extracurricular activities

October/November

- Take the PSAT examination at your school

- Talk to your parent/guardian about college

December

- It's important to request information from colleges over the internet because some will make the application free.

- Research and identify a summer job or a summer college prep program

January/February

- Continue to prepare for the SAT by purchasing a SAT study book

- Make certain that you have registered for the SAT or SAT II by February for the April test

Research Scholarships

- March/April

- Visit colleges

- Register by March in preparation for the May SAT

- May/June/July

- Send for the scholarship applications

- Compile your personal materials including a resume, writing samples, video tapes admission to college

- Participate in a summer program or take a college course

12th Grade Check List

September

- Buy another calendar which you will use to keep track of important assignments

- Buy another folder to keep all of your college materials

- Register during September for the October or November SAT

October/November

- Complete college applications

- Talk to your parent/guardian about college

- Write your essays for your college application

December

- Make sure that you complete all applications on time

- Make sure that you have all teacher and counselor recommendations

January

- Complete the Free Application for Federal Student Aid (FAFSA)

- Review and submit college applications

February/March

- Make sure that your report cards where sent to colleges

- Call or e-mail admissions offices to ensure that your admissions material is in the office

April/May/June/July

- Compile your file of materials received from colleges

- Get ready for college and participate in a summer program if it is available

- Continue to apply for scholarships throughout Your college enrollment

APPENDIX

Career Resources

If you are looking for information about careers, browse through the following links for some exciting career information!

College Resources

These websites will help you to identify additional resources to help your student

The Kiplinger website provides information to help parents to design a college financial plan

- Thomas Peterson's college and graduate school planning

- College information

- College information website

- College search engine

Greater Washington College Information Center

- College catalogue resource

- College admission counselor website

- College information for home schoolers

- College information and publication

- College Information 2005

The internet Guide for Funding College

- Links to colleges around the world

- College and information sites

- College information database

- College web

APPENDIX

Youth Organization List

Upward Bound- www.ed.gov/programs/trioupbound

Gear Up- www.ed.gov/gearup

YMCA-www.ymca.net

Talent Search- www.ed.gov/programs/triotalent

YWCA-www.ywca.org

Inroads-www.inroads.org

Upward Bound Math and Science- www.ed.gov/programs/trioupbound

Society for Hispanic Professional Engineers-www.shpe.org

National Society of Black Engineers-www.nsbe.org

Boy Scouts of America-www.bsa.scouting.org

Girl Scouts of America-www.Girlscouts.org

Philadelphia Youth Network-www.pyninc.org

City Year-www.city-year.org

United Way-www.uwint.org

Camp Fire Girls and Boys-www.campfireusa.org

Big Brothers Big Sisters of America-www.bbbsa.org

ASPIRA Inc. – www.Aspira.org

Boys and Girls Club of America-www.bgca.org

Girls Incorporated-www.girlsinc.com

National 4h Council –www.fourhconcil.edu

National Parent Teacher Association – www.pta.org

National Storytelling Network-www.storynet.org

21 Ways to Find A Summer Job

1. Call your school counselor's office.

2. Visit or call your local legislator's office.

3. Call the personnel office at your job.

4. Go onto the internet and conduct a search for a summer job in your city.

5. Start as a volunteer at a hospital or business

6. Call your superintendents office to ask about summer jobs and internships.

7. Help your son/daughter to create a resume that he/she can distribute to family and friends.

8. Call your schools superintendent's office.

9. Contact companies in the employment section of your newspaper.

10. Start a job at a local McDonald etc..

11. Help your son/daughter to start their own business so that they can demonstrate their management skills.

12. Call your local colleges to ask about research programs for high school students. Try calling the engineering, chemistry, biology or computer science department.

13. Ask your local college about pre-college programs.

14. Visit the library and research summer jobs in your area.
Talk with the librarian to identify specific books.

15. Go onto a radio program and let people know that you are looking for a job.

16. Talk to someone at your city hall about summer youth employment.

APPENDIX

17. Join an organization that offers jobs as a part of the training.

18. Talk to a member of a sorority or a fraternity about internships and summer jobs. Ask if they have any members who have previously offered jobs to students.

19. Write a letter to your local newspaper about your quest to find a job for your student.

20. Organize a few friends who will also help you to search for a summer job.

21. Talk to members of your church or religious organization.

Notes

APPENDIX

Scholarship Websites

100 Free Scholarships

1   Intel Science Talent Search
    www.1sciserv.org/sts

2   FinAid: The Smart Students Guide to
    Financial Aid (scholarships)
    www.finaid.org/scholarships/

3   Broke Scholars Scholarships
    www.scholarships.brokesscholar.com

4   LULAC - National Scholastic Achievement Awards
    www.mach25.collegenet.com

5   Paralegal Scholarships
    www.paralegals.org

6   Science Net Scholarship Listing
    www.sciencenet.emory.edu

7   Siemens Foundation Competition
    www.siemens-foundation.org

8   College Board Scholarship Search
    www.cbweb10p.collegeboard.org

9   International Students Scholarships & Aid Help
    www.iefa.org

10 Guaranteed Scholarships
    www.guaranteed-scholarships.com

11 Hope Scholarships and Lifetime Learning Credits
    www.ed.gov/offices

12 Presidential Freedom Scholarships
    www.nationalservice.org/scholarships

13 Sports Scholarships and Internships
    www.ncaa.org/about/scholarships

APPENDIX

Scholarship Websites

100 Free Scholarships continued

14   Student Video Scholarships
http://www.christophers.org/vidcon2k.html

15   Student Inventors Scholarships
http://www.invent.org/collegiate/

16   Decca Scholarships
http://www.deca.org/scholarships/

17   Scholarships Pathways

18   Private Scholarships For Seniors
http://www.phs.d211.org/stsvc/college/scholarships.asp

19   Science Net Scholarship Listing
http://www.sciencenet.emory.edu/undergrad/scholarships.html

20   Chela Education Financing "Gateway to Success Scholarship"
http://www.loans4students.org

21   Princeton Review Scholarships & Aid
http://www.princetonreview.com/college/finance

22   American Legion Scholarships
http://www.legion.org

23   Free Scholarship Search
http://www.srnexpress.com

24   2005 Holocaust Remembrance Essay Contest
http://www.holocaust.hklaw.com

25   Horace Mann Scholarship Program
http://www.horacemann.com/scholarship

APPENDIX

Scholarship Websites

100 Free Scholarships continued

26 Ayn Rand Institute
http://www.aynrand.org/contests

27 The David and Dovetta Wilson Scholarship Fund
http://www.wilsonfund.org

28 Congressional Hispanic Scholarships
http://www.chciyouth.org

29 Nursing Scholarships
http://www.blackexcel.org/nursing-scholarships.html

30 College-Bound High School Seniors - Scholarships
http://scholarships.fatomei.com/scholar13.html

31 AFROTC High School Scholarships
http://www.afrotc.com/

32 The Elks National Foundation Scholarships
http://www.elks.org/enf/scholars/ourscholarships.cfm

33 Art Deadlines and Scholarships
http://www.xensei.com/users/adl/

34 Journalism Grants
http://www.mccormicktribune.org/journalism/grantslist.htm

35 Marine Corps Scholarships
http://www.marine-scholars.org/

36 Research for Women & Minorities Underrepresented in the Sciences
http://www.research.att.com/academic/urp.html

37 Tylenol Scholarships
http://scholarship.tylenol.com/

APPENDIX

Scholarship Websites

100 Free Scholarships continued

38   Undergraduate Scholarships (Health)
http://ugsp.info.nih.gov/InfoUGSP.htm

39   State Farm Insurance Hispanic Scholarships
http://www.statefarm.com/foundati/hispanic.htm

40   National Scholarships at All Levels
http://scholarships.fatomei.com/

41   Burger King Scholars (Annual Awards)
http://www.bk.com/CompanyInfo/community/BKscholars/index.aspx

42   Ambassadorial Scholarships
http://www.rotary.org/foundation/educational/amb_scho/

43   Baptist Scholarships
http://www.free-4u.com/baptist_scholarships.htm

44   Methodist Scholarships
http://www.free-4u.com/methodist_scholarships.htm

45   Project Excellence Scholarships
http://www.project-excellence.com

46   Discover Card Tribute Award Scholarships
http://www.aasa.org/Discover.htm

47   United States National Peace Essay Contest
http://www.usip.org/ed/npec/index.shtml

48   Gateway to 10 Free Scholarship Searches
http://www.college-scholarships.com/free_scholarship_searches.htm

49   Accounting Scholarships
http://www.aicpa.org/members/div/career/edu/jlcs.htm

Appendix

APPENDIX

Scholarship Websites

100 Free Scholarships continued

50   Americorps
http://www.cns.gov/

51   Sports Scholarships and Internships
http://www.ncaa.org/about/scholarships.html

52   100 Minority Scholarship Gateways
http://www.blackexcel.org/100minority.htm

53   Awards and Scholarships
http://www-hl.syr.edu/cas-pages/ScholarshipsAvailable.htm

54   American Chemical Society Scholarships
http://www.cnetweb.org/american_chemical_society_scholarships.htm

55   Sallie Mae Grants and Scholarships
http://www.salliemae.com/parent_answer/decide/

56   Scholarships List and Search
http://www.adventuresineducation.org/sbase/

57   New York State Scholarships for Academic Excellence
http://www.hesc.com/bulletin.nsf/

58   Hispanic Scholarship Fund
http://www.hsf.net/

59   Scholarship Research Center: US NEWS
http://12.47.197.196/usnews/

60   Pacific Northwest Scholarship Guide Online
http://fp2.adhost.com/collegeplan/scholarship/default.asp

61   College Net Scholarship Search
http://mach25.collegenet.com/cgi-bin/M25/index

APPENDIX

Scholarship Websites

100 Free Scholarships continued

62   Scholarships For Hispanics
http://www.scholarshipsforhispanics.org/

63   National Federation of the Blind Scholarships
http://www.nfb.org/services/schlprg02.htm

64   Actuary Scholarships for Minority Students
http://www.beanactuary.org/minority/

65   Astronaut Scholarship Foundation
http://www.astronautscholarship.org/

66   ELA Foundation Scholarships (disabled)
http://www.ela.org/scholarships/scholarships.html

67   Indian Health Service Scholarships
http://www.ihs.gov/JobsCareerDevelop/DHPS/SP/spTOC.asp

68   Minority Undergraduate Fellows Program
http://www.naspa.org/resources/mufp/

69   Third Wave Foundation Scholarships
http://www.thirdwavefoundation.org/programs/scholarships.html

70   College Connection Scholarships
http://www.collegescholarships.com/

71   Super College Scholarships
http://www.supercollege.com

72   Indian Students
http://www.gurgaonscoop.com/story/2005/3/14/195141/137

73   Comprehensive Recourse List (All cultures)
http://www.globalvision.org/educate/connected/sect4e.html

APPENDIX

Scholarship Websites

100 Free Scholarships continued

74 Scholarship Database (Alphabetical Listing)
http://www.campuscareercenter.com/scholarships/scholarships.asp

75 Music Scholarships
http://www.newenglandconservatory.edu/

76 Navy Scholarship Lists
http://www.odu.edu/ao/hrnrotc/scholarship/scholarships.htm

77 National Assoc. of Black Journalists Scholarships (NABJ)
http://www.nabj.org/programs/scholarships/index.html

78 Science and Engineering Student Scholarships
http://www.bell-labs.com/fellowships/

79 The Roothbert Fund Scholarships
http://www.roothbertfund.org/scholarships.php

80 Gateway to 10 Free Scholarship Searches
http://www.college-scholarships.com/free_scholarship_searches.htm

81 Federal Scholarships and Aid
http://www.fedmoney.org/

82 International Students Help and Scholarships
http://www.iefa.org/

83 NACME Scholarship Program
http://www.nacme.org/scholarships/

84 Black Excel Scholarship Gateway
http://www.blackexcel.org/link4.htm

85 Peterson's Aid and Scholarships Help
http://www.petersons.com/finaid/

APPENDIX

Scholarship Websites

100 Free Scholarships continued

86   Alpha Kappa Alpha Scholarships
http://www.akaeaf.org/scholarships.htm

87   Coveted National Scholarships
http://scholarships.fatomei.com/

88   25 Scholarship Gateways from Black Excel
http://www.blackexcel.org/25scholarships.htm

89   Martin Luther King Scholarships
http://www.sanantonio.gov/mlk/?res=1024&ver=true

90   Financial Aid Research Center
http://www.theoldschool.org/

91   Art and Writing Awards
http://www.artandwriting.org

92   Wells Fargo Scholarships
http://www.wellsfargo.com/collegesteps

93   Princeton Review Internships
http://www.princetonreview.com/cte/search/internshipAdvSearch.asp

94   Chicana/Latina Foundation
http://www.chicanalatina.org/scholarship.html

95   NCAA Scholarships and Internships
http://www.ncaa.org/about/scholarships.html

96   Congressional Hispanic Caucus Institute
http://www.chci.org/

97   Morris K. Udall Foundation Scholarships
http://www.udall.gov/p_scholarship.asp

APPENDIX

Scholarship Websites

100 Free Scholarships continued

Notes

Tips Parents of College Bound Students Must Know

In the beginning:

- Spend special time communicating with your child, and encourage him to reflect on his or her academic strengths as well as personal strengths and weaknesses.

- Discuss the benefits and costs of living on campus and living at home.

- Enroll your student in a SAT/ACT preparation course. Your student will be better prepared for the test. Also, consider purchasing computer software that they can use to get immediate feedback on their SAT/ACT knowledge.

- Go onto the internet and visit websites of various colleges.This will give you and your child an opportunity to learn about a specific college or university, and decide if you want to learn more and/or visit the school in person.

Money and expenses:

- It's never too early to begin saving for college.

- Set up a bank account for your child and put as much savings in it as possible.

- If expenses are an issue, consider the option of community college. Attending community college for 2 years before transferring to a 4 year college or university will save a significant amount of money.

Scholarships and financial aid:

- Finding scholarships are easier than you think, but you should start researching available scholarships before your child's junior year of high school.

- As you collect information about what is available, categorize scholarships by deadlines and qualifications.

- Encourage your child to apply for some unusual scholarships, e.g. scholarships for left-handed people, musicians, artists, etc.

- All parents, regardless of income, should complete the federal financial aid form, called the FAFSA. You can obtain it ion the internet, or in your child's high school guidance counselor's office.

Tips Parents of College Bound Students Must Know

The application process:

- Together with your child, make a list of the top five or so colleges and universities of interest, and try to plan campus visits by geographic regions.

- Visit the schools that are on your child's priority list, and take advantage of any introductory programs they provide, e.g. open houses, information sessions, meeting with a faculty member, attending class with a current student.

- Try to visit as many colleges and universities as possible during your child's junior year of high school. Your child should use the fall of his or her senior year to fill out applications.

- If a friend or relative graduated from a college or university that your child is applying to, you might want to ask him or her to write a letter of recommendation on behalf of your child.

Getting ready for college:

- Find out if your child's college or university encourages its students to purchase a specific computer or laptop, and what technical support the school provides to its students. Some schools include a computer in their tuition package and want all students to have the same computer; therefore, it is imperative that you research this before you go out and purchase a computer on your own.

- If your child decides to attend a college away from home, identify a relative or friend nearby. Having a local family contact is important in case there is an emergency.

- Many colleges and universities offer students an opportunity to meet their roommates before they arrive on campus. Encourage your child to contact his or her roommate(s) so they can get acquainted before they move in, and so they can coordinate the items they will bring for their dorm room. If possible, meet the roommate's parents so you can both be active participants in your child's adjustment to college life.

- If your child knows what classes he or she will be tacking for the first semester and is able to find out what books he or she will need, your child should purchase the books early. Buying textbooks online is a lot cheaper then buying them in the school's bookstore.

- Avoid the temptation to over pack. Dorm rooms are small and they can only hold a few large items, such as a mini regrigerator, television and computer.

Tips Parents of College Bound Students Must Know

Once on campus:

- Write down the names of college administrators you meet during new student orientation.

- Remind your child to avoid the temptation to sign up for credit cards when they arrive on campus, because these credit cards can have very high interest rates.

- If you anticipate that your child might have a need for tutoring in a particular discipline, make sure you are aware of the academic support that is available on campus, and encourage your child to take advantage of what is available.

Notes